Bristo st!

Frank Dickens

Abelard-Schuman London

An Evening Standard Book

Bristow : Frank Dickens

Gentle reader,
After its winter sojourn in the sun this bird has lost its homing instinct and, confused and bewildered flies hither and thither....

CRAAK!
CRAAK!

If it could speak it would be crying "Where am I? Where am I?"

CRAAK!
CRAAK!

Is there no salvation; or is he, like the Flying Dutchman, doomed to travel the world forever?

BRISTOW — GET ON WITH YOUR WORK!

CLICK!

CHIRRUP! CHIRRUP!

4369

Bristow : Frank Dickens

WELL, I'LL BE — IF IT ISN'T MY FEATHERED FRIEND WINGING HIS WEARY WAY BACK FROM HIS SOJOURN IN THE SUN....

FLAP! FLAP!
FLAP! FLAP!
FLAP!
FLAP!

HALLO, OLD CHAP.... WELCOME BACK! I DIDN'T EXPECT TO SEE YOU FOR **AGES**

GASP!

WE HAVEN'T HAD ANY WHAT YOU MIGHT CALL REAL BAD WEATHER UP TO NOW.... WE'VE GOT IT ALL TO COME...

SIGH!

FLAP! FLAP! FLAP! FLAP! FLAP!

4330A

Bristow : Frank Dickens

COME ALONG, DUANE DEAR — YOU DON'T WANT TO BE LATE ON YOUR FIRST DAY AT WORK, DO YOU?

TUG! TUG!

I DON'T WANT TO GO TO WORK!

DON'T LET'S GO THROUGH ALL THAT AGAIN... YOU'RE GOING TO WORK AND THAT'S IT!

TUG! TUG!

BUT MUM —!

THAT'S ENOUGH....

I DON'T WANT TO GO TO WORK IN THE NASTY HORRIBLE ROTTEN CHESTER-PERRY BUILDING

YOU AND ME BOTH, KID......

Bristow: Frank Dickens

....AND THIS NEXT OFFICE IS THE BUYING DEPARTMENT — THREE TEAS, ONE WITHOUT SUGAR....

BRISTOW — HOW MANY TIMES DO YOU HAVE TO BE TOLD, YOU INCOMPETENT, BUNGLING WRETCH! GET ON WITH YOUR WORK!!! IF I CATCH YOU SLACKING ONCE MORE YOU'LL BE SORRY AND THAT'S A PROMISE......

COME AWAY FROM THERE, ELIZABETH...

I CAN'T BEAR TO SEE GROWN MEN SHOUTING AT EACH OTHER.....

4233

Bristow: Frank Dickens

I'VE GOT TO HAND IT TO YOU, BRISTOW — YOU WERE MAGNIFICENT...

I'VE NEVER HEARD FUDGE GIVING ANYONE SUCH A DRESSING DOWN IN PUBLIC...

WAVE UPON WAVE OF INVECTIVE DELIVERED AT THE TOP OF HIS VOICE AND YOU DIDN'T BAT AN EYELID....

YOU STOOD THERE WITH YOUR EYES LOWERED AND YOUR FISTS LIGHTLY CLENCHED, TOTALLY OBLIVIOUS TO ANYTHING HE MIGHT HAVE SAID... HOW DID YOU DO IT?

EASY PEASY...

I GOT THE IDEA FROM SOMEONE I ONCE SAW OPERATING A PNEUMATIC DRILL.......

4234

Bristow: Frank Dickens

MR. BRISTOW — I NEED YOUR HOLIDAY DATES PLEASE....

MISS SUNMAN — YOU SHOULD KNOW BY NOW IT'S NOT UP TO ME... ASK THE HEAD OF MY DEPARTMENT WHEN I CAN BEST BE SPARED

I ALREADY DID....

WELL, WHAT DID HE SAY?

HE SAID HE CAN SPARE YOU ANY TIME...

SOB!

4326

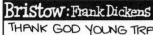

Bristow: Frank Dickens

THANK GOD YOUNG TRAYNOR'S GONE...
HE'S FAIR WORN ME OUT WITH HIS
MERRY QUIPS AND JOKES.....

I'D LIKE TO KNOW WHERE HE GETS THEM ALL FROM...

MEANWHILE: IN AN ANTIQUE
BOOKSHOP NOT FAR AWAY....

PROP: B. STONE

TURRET BOOKSHO

WELL, MR. TRAYNOR — I'VE MANAGED TO
OBTAIN ANOTHER COPY OF "CHICK'S OWN"
TWO COPIES OF "CHIPS" TWO COPIES OF
"FILM FUN" AND HALF A DOZEN "BEANOS"...

4310

Bristow: Frank Dickens

I DON'T KNOW WHY WE HAVE
THIS RIDICULOUS PANTOMIME
EVERY TIME I COME ROUND
ASKING FOR WEDDING PRESENT
DONATIONS...

IT ISN'T AS IF I'M ASKING
FOR THE MOON... TEN PENCE
DOESN'T HURT ANYBODY...

AFTER ALL, HE KNOWS
THE GIRL... SHE'S TYPED
HIS WORK OUT OFTEN
ENOUGH.....

COO-EE MR. B.....
COO-EE

4141

Bristow: Frank Dickens

DID YOU CLEAR THAT LAST
ORDER WITH GUN & FAMES?

YES MR FUDGE — THE ITEMS
WERE DELIVERED THIS MORNING..

GRUNT!
WELL DONE

PRAISE!! PRAISE
AT LAST!!!!

AFTER YEARS SPENT
IN THE WILDERNESS.......

4354

Bristow : Frank Dickens

FUNNY REALLY, HOW MY LIFE SEEMS TO HAVE TAKEN A TURN FOR THE BETTER....

A FEW KIND WORDS FROM OLD FUDGE AND SUDDENLY I'M THE BUYING CLERK WHO CAME IN OUT OF THE COLD.....

FOR THE FIRST TIME I'M SNUG AND WARM, WELL WRAPPED UP IN THE BLANKET OF CHESTER-PERRY APPROVAL....

STOP DAYDREAMING! — GET ON WITH YOUR WORK!!!

HEIGH HO FOR THE GREAT OUTDOORS.....

4358

Bristow : Frank Dickens

...AND NOW A TRAFFIC REPORT...

MOTORISTS ON THE NORTHBOUND CARRIAGEWAY ARE ADVISED OF A FIVE MILE TRAFFIC JAM CAUSED BY A CHESTER-PERRY LORRY OVERTURNING...

DRIVERS TRAVELLING **SOUTH** ARE WARNED OF A TWO MILE TAIL-BACK OWING TO A CHESTER-PERRY LORRY WHICH HAS JACKNIFED.

MOTORISTS MAKING FOR THE **WESTERN** TUNNEL ARE ADVISED TO SEEK ALTERNATIVE ROUTES AS THE TUNNEL IS BLOCKED BY A CHESTER-PERRY LORRY WHICH HAS BROKEN DOWN...

ON THE **EASTBOUND** CARRIAGEWAY CONSIDERABLE DELAYS CAN BE EXPECTED DUE TO A CHESTER-PERRY LORRY SHEDDING ITS LOAD.....

4341

Bristow : Frank Dickens

YOU CAN SET YOUR WATCH BY ME...

SPOT ON SEVEN THIRTY I WAKE UP... SEVEN FORTY FIVE I'M SHAVED, BREAKFASTED AND READY TO GO.....

EIGHT O'CLOCK PROMPT SEES ME PACING THE PLATFORM...

AND NINE O'CLOCK SEES ME WALKING INTO MY OFFICE...

CREATURE OF HABIT, THAT'S ME...

NINE FIFTEEN —HARD AT IT...

NINE THIRTY...

4310 A

Bristow: Frank Dickens

YOU NEVER CEASE TO SURPRISE ME, BRISTOW. GIVING THAT MOTORIST A PUSH START UP THAT HILL... LOOK AT YOU NOW, EXHAUSTED AND DIRTY — WHY DID YOU DO IT?

GASP!

WELL, JONES, I ALWAYS REMEMBER THE STORY OF ANDROCLES AND THE LION...

HE PULLED A THORN OUT OF A LION'S PAW AND YEARS LATER THE LION REPAID HIM BY NOT EATING HIM IN THE ARENA...

ONE NEVER KNOWS WHETHER A SIMPLE ACT OF KINDNESS WILL REBOUND....

SEE — HERE COMES THAT VERY MOTORIST... PROBABLY TO OFFER ME A LIFT — CHEERIO, JONES...

SORRY TO TROUBLE YOU AGAIN, BUT IT STALLED AT THE TRAFFIC LIGHTS. ......

4255

Bristow: Frank Dickens

Scene: The Personnel Department of the monolithic Chester-Perry organisation....

GET ON WITH IT!

SO DALRYMPLE HAS BEEN WITH THE FIRM TWENTY-FIVE YEARS — I TAKE IT WE'LL BE MAKING A PRESENTATION TOMORROW?

TOMORROW AT TWELVE

WILL THAT GIVE US TIME TO HAVE A GOLD WATCH ENGRAVED?

GOLD WATCH MY FOOT!

FOR TWENTY-FIVE YEARS IT'S A **BOOK TOKEN** OR **RECORD VOUCHER**........

4160

Bristow: Frank Dickens

I HEAR YOU'VE BEEN WITH THE FIRM TWENTY-FIVE YEARS TOMORROW

DON'T REMIND ME.... TWENTY-FIVE BORING YEARS.....

LOOK AT IT OUT THERE... A BEAUTIFUL DAY AND I'M STUCK IN THIS STUFFY OFFICE...

OPEN YOUR WINDOW

NO FEAR

I NEVER OPEN THAT — EVEN IN THE HOTTEST WEATHER I KEEP IT FIRMLY CLOSED...

WITH IT OPEN I MIGHT BE SEIZED BY AN UNCONTROLLABLE URGE TO THROW MYSELF OUT!

4162

Bristow: Frank Dickens

SO, AS EDITOR OF THE HOUSE JOURNAL YOU PUT A LOT OF YOURSELF INTO THE MAGAZINE?

I SUPPOSE YOU **COULD** SAY THAT, REALLY

I VOICE A GREAT MANY OPINIONS AND, WITHOUT BEING IMMODEST, MAKE A GREAT NUMBER OF PEOPLE SQUIRM....

THE PEN IS MIGHTIER THAN THE SWORD, REMEMBER, HO! HO! HO!

MIND YOU — I DON'T GO AS FAR AS TO PUT MY JOB IN JEOPARDY.....!

I SEE...

IN YOUR CASE THE PEN IS MIGHTIER THAN THE SWORD BUT NOT HALF AS MIGHTY AS THE AXE...... HO! HO! HO! HO!

4079

Bristow: Frank Dickens

IF ONLY YOU COULD SPEAK, WHAT TALES YOU COULD TELL...

I SAY, BRISTOW —

SQUAWK!

NOW LOOK WHAT YOU'VE DONE, JONES...

WONDER WHY HE ALWAYS FLIES AWAY WHEN HE SEES ME?

HE'S TERRIFIED OF YOU......
IT'S THE WAY YOU LOOK AT HIM....

AS THOUGH YOU SEE HIM ON A PLATE WITH A SALAD ON THE SIDE.......

4349A

Bristow: Frank Dickens

GOOD MORNING, MISS SUNMAN. I'D LIKE TO SPEAK TO THE NEW GIRL...

YOU MEAN MISS COLLINGS? CERTAINLY

MISS COLLINGS, I HAVE SOME CORRESPONDENCE HERE FOR GUN AND FAMES AND I'D LIKE YOU TO HANDLE IT.... GUN & FAMES ALWAYS PRESENT A CHALLENGE

I'M NOT VERY FAST I'M AFRAID — I ONLY STARTED HERE THIS MORNING

EXACTLY... AND THAT'S WHY I'VE COME TO YOU FOR A FRESH APPROACH AS IT WERE.. A NEW **MIND** ON THE PROBLEM, SO TO SPEAK..

LAST TIME I USED **MIRROR** WRITING... THE TIME BEFORE THAT UPSIDE DOWN BACK TO FRONT..... THE TIME BEFORE **THAT** INVISIBLE INK...........

4348

Bristow: Frank Dickens

~SIGH!~

IT'S NO USE....

I KEEP THINKING OF **THE GORGEOUS MISS PRETTY OF KLEENAPHONE**...

HARD TO IMAGINE MY BEING SMITTEN BY A YOUNG SLIP OF A GIRL BUT THERE'S NO DOUBT— I **AM**...

I CAN'T **SLEEP**.... I CAN'T **EAT**... I CAN'T DO **INVOICING**... CAN'T DO **FILING**... CAN'T **DICTATE**... CAN'T OPEN ANY **LETTERS**.......................

4292

Bristow: Frank Dickens

I SEE YOU'RE DOING WELL WITH THE GORGEOUS MISS PRETTY OF KLEENAPHONE...

I DON'T KNOW SO MUCH

BUT AS SHE WAS CLEANING YOUR PHONE I SAW HER FLUTTER HER EYELASHES..

THEN I SAW HER REACH FOR YOUR HAND....

DUST IN HER EYES

I HAPPENED TO BE HOLDING THE RECEIVER AND SHE WANTED TO CLEAN IT

THEN SHE WRINKLED HER NOSE —

HEAVY HANDED WITH THE DISINFECTANT...

AND WHAT WAS ALL THAT NODDING BEFORE SHE LEFT?

SHE HAD HER NECK CAUGHT UP IN THE CABLE AND WAS TRYING TO FREE HERSELF.....

4295

Bristow: Frank Dickens

MR. GORDON BLUE— WHAT SHALL WE DO?

THE CANTEEN IS CROWDED BUT THERE IS NO TOMATO SAUCE ON THE TABLES....

TEE HEE— MY PLAN IS WORKING... I HAVE ALLOWED OUR STOCKS OF THAT VILE CONCOCTION TO RUN DOWN SO THAT MY HUNGRY CLIENTELE SHALL ENJOY THE TASTE OF PURE FOOD SUPERBLY COOKED....

BUT THEY ARE SEATED AT THEIR TABLES SWEATING PROFUSELY, THEIR HANDS TREMBLING, THEIR EYES STARTING WILDLY FROM THEIR HEADS

SACRE NOM DE DIEU! THE ONE THING EVERY CHEF DREADS...

TOMATO KETCHUP WITHDRAWAL SYMPTOMS...

4364

Bristow: Frank Dickens

THIS FUNBOY BROCHURE IS MAGNIFICENT.... MARVELLOUS PHOTOGRAPHS!

FUNBOYS SUR LA PLAGE.. AH, YES... NOSTALGIA....

WHAT A GREAT HOLIDAY THAT WAS.... BEST I'VE EVER HAD....

THERE'S THE TAHITI DINING ROOM WHERE THE WAITER SPILT SCALDING COFFEE IN MY LAP.....

THERE'S THE CLIFF WALK WHERE I WAS STRUCK ON THE HEAD BY A LOW SLUNG CABLE CAR...

THERE'S THE SWIMMING POOL THE HOTEL STAFF **THREW** ME IN FULLY CLOTHED ON THE DAY I LEFT.....

4330

Bristow: Frank Dickens

IT'LL BE A FULL HOUSE TODAY, MABEL — IT'S RAINING CATS AND DOGS OUT THERE......

WHERE'S OUR MASTER CHEF, MR. GORDON BLUE?

HE'S GONE INTO HIDING WITH A BOTTLE OF COOKING SHERRY...

HE DIDN'T ANTICIPATE THIS WEATHER WHEN HE PREPARED TODAY'S MENU....

WATERCRESS SOUP, **RAIN**BOW TROUT, **POO**LET EN COCOTTE WITH **SPRING** ONIONS, **MACK**ERONI CHEESE AND WATER ICES....

WOT! NO BREAD AND DRIPPING?

EAU DEAR!

MENU, MENU GO AWAY COME AGAIN ANOTHER DAY

4222

Bristow: Frank Dickens

'MORNING, GENTLEMEN...

'MORNING, MR.B — JUST IN TIME FOR TEA...

DON'T ENCOURAGE HIM TO STAY... WE SEE ENOUGH OF HIS TYPE AT LUNCH TIMES...

LIKE A PACK OF WILD ANIMALS, PUSHING AND SHOVING... TAKES US THE BEST PART OF OUR LUNCH HOUR TO GET ANYWHERE NEAR THE COUNTER, LET ALONE GET SERVED....

I'VE NEVER SEEN YOU IN THE CANTEEN...

WHO'S TALKING ABOUT THE CANTEEN?

I'M TALKING ABOUT THE NEW BETTING SHOP ON THE CORNER!

4244

Bristow: Frank Dickens

I DON'T KNOW WHY YOU'RE SO UPTIGHT ABOUT THE BETTING SHOP ON THE CORNER...

RACING IS, AFTER ALL, THE SPORT OF KINGS...

EVEN OUR BELOVED FIRM'S FOUNDER, SIR REGINALD CHESTER-PERRY HAS A STRING OF HORSES

REALLY?

CERTAINLY — HE'S A PASSIONATE RACEGOER.

AS A MATTER OF FACT IT WAS SIR REGINALD HIMSELF WHO DESIGNED THE CHESTER-PERRY RACING COLOURS....

PINSTRIPED SHIRT WITH **WHITE** COLLAR AND CUFFS, **CARBON PAPER** BLUE CROSSBELTS AND **CLERICAL GREY** CAP......

4247

Bristow: Frank Dickens

WHEN YOU SAY THINGS ARE TIGHTENING UP ON THE SWITCHBOARD, WHAT DO YOU MEAN?

ALL CALLS TO BE VETTED? FINE... NO PROBLEM AT ALL..

PUT ME THROUGH TO MESSRS GUN & FAMES PLEASE... OF COURSE IT'S A BUSINESS CALL

ANSWER A FEW QUESTIONS? WITH PLEASURE.... FIRE AWAY...

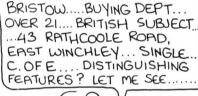

BRISTOW.....BUYING DEPT... OVER 21....BRITISH SUBJECT...
...43 RATHCOOLE ROAD, EAST WINCHLEY... SINGLE... C. OF E.... DISTINGUISHING FEATURES? LET ME SEE......

4366

Bristow: Frank Dickens

STANDING ON THE CORNER WATCHING ALL THE GIRLS GO BY...

TYPISTS..

SECRETARIES...

TELEPHONISTS.....

4368

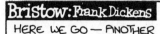

Bristow: Frank Dickens

HERE WE GO — ANOTHER LAZY DAY....

MAKING A GRAND TOTAL OF FIVE IN A ROW....

CROSSWORD... PACKET OF BISCUITS..... SETTLE DOWN AND WAIT FOR TEABREAK...

W.J. TURNER? NEVER HEARD OF HIM

AH, THERE YOU ARE BRISTOW.... A MR. W.J. TURNER HAS BEEN LOOKING FOR YOU EVERYWHERE

CHESTER-PERRY WHO'S WHO

TAYLOR... TRULOVE... TURNBULL... AH! HERE WE ARE—

HOLY MACKEREL! W.J. TURNER —THE FIRM'S HATCHET MAN !!

GULP!

4238

Bristow: Frank Dickens

WHERE'S BRISTOW THIS MORNING ?

SEARCH ME...

EVER SINCE HE LEARNED THAT W.J. TURNER, THE FIRM'S HATCHET MAN WAS LOOKING FOR HIM HE SEEMS TO HAVE DISAPPEARED OFF THE FACE OF THE EARTH...

WHY ON EARTH DOES TURNER WANT TO SEE BRISTOW ?

DUNNO. BRISTOW DIDN'T STAY LONG ENOUGH TO FIND OUT. HE JUST VANISHED...

YOU HAVEN'T SEEN ME.....

4239

Bristow: Frank Dickens

O.K — THE CHIPS ARE DOWN...

IF W.J. TURNER, THE FIRM'S HATCHET MAN IS LOOKING FOR ME, THEN LET HIM <u>FIND</u> ME...

WHEN IT COMES TO THE NITTY GRITTIES WE BRISTOWS WALK TALL...

♪ WHO'S AFRAID OF THE BIG BAD WOLF..? ♪

BRISTOW—THERE'S A MAN WITH STEELY BLUE EYES WAITING BY YOUR DESK...

STEELY BLUE EYES, EH? THAT SOUNDS LIKE W.J. TURNER....

MR. BRISTOW ?

ER...YES — I MEAN ER...NO.... I MEAN-ER... WHAT DO YOU WANT ME TO SAY...?

4240

Bristow: Frank Dickens

TELL YOU WHAT, JASON — I FEEL IN A SILLY MOOD TODAY — LET US HAVE SOME SPORT.....

TEE HEE

OBSERVE THIS TARDY COMMUTER... CONFIDENTLY EXPECTING TO BOARD THIS TRAIN. METHINKS OUR SPORT IS ABOUT TO COMMENCE.....

NOW?? **NOW??**

HOLD HARD — WAIT UNTIL HE ACTUALLY HAS THE DOOR OPEN

HIS HAND REACHES OUT... HE OPENS THE DOOR... HE RAISES ONE FOOT ——

GO, MAN, GO!!!

YIPPEE!

4359

Bristow: Frank Dickens

The story so far:
Two mischievous employees of British Hi-Speed rail are enjoying themselves at the expense of a commuter.....

SNIGGER!

WHAT FUN IT IS TO SEE THE LOOK OF CONSTERNATION ON THE FACE OF A WOULD-BE PASSENGER WHEN WE ACCELERATE AT THE VERY MOMENT HE ATTEMPTS TO BOARD THE TRAIN

TEE HEE — SUCH FUN WE SELDOM SEE

OBSERVE HIM NOW — HIS HAND GRIPPING THE DOOR HANDLE — HIS LEGS A BLUR — HIS FEET SCARCE TOUCHING THE GROUND

SNIGGER!

BUT WAIT! HE GRITS HIS TEETH... HE RELEASES THE HANDLE OF THE DOOR

WHAT THE HELL DO YOU TWO THINK YOU'RE PLAYING AT?

4360

Bristow: Frank Dickens

4361

HELLO, HELLO, HELLO — WHAT'S GOING ON IN THE STATIONMASTERS OFFICE?

APPARENTLY SOME KIND OF KANGAROO COURT IS BEING HELD.....

SOME LUCKLESS COMMUTER IS UP ON TWO CHARGES....
Ⓐ OPENING THE DOOR WHILST THE TRAIN IS IN MOTION...
Ⓑ ATTEMPTING TO BOARD A MOVING TRAIN....

POOR DEVIL — THAT'LL COST HIM A FEW BOB......

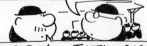

SSH! STATIONMASTER IS NOW SUMMING UP..

STATION MASTER

PRAY SILENCE.......
JUDGEMENT OF THIS COURT.... **GUILTY**... BOTH CHARGES... THE SUM OF TEN POUNDS....PLUS

SEASON TICKET ENDORSED TWICE!

SOB!

MAN'S INHUMANITY TO MAN...

THERE, BUT FOR THE GRACE....

Bristow: Frank Dickens

FUNNY, REALLY, OUR PATHS CROSSING AFTER ALL THESE YEARS...

DO YOU REALISE IF I HADN'T BEEN INSPIRED BY YOUR DETERMINATION TO BE A BRAIN SURGEON I'D NEVER HAVE HAD THE COURAGE TO LEAVE EFFANDEE HOLDINGS AND SET UP ON MY OWN...?

I'VE DRAGGED MYSELF UP FROM BEING A SIMPLE BUYING CLERK TO OWNER OF A FLEET OF ICE CREAM VANS AND I OWE IT ALL TO YOU.

WELL, ER... I MUST BE GOING... ER.. HOW MUCH FOR THE ICE CREAM?

PLEASE, DOCTOR — DO ME A FAVOUR — PUT YOUR MONEY AWAY..........

4.103

Bristow: Frank Dickens

FANCY YOUNG TAYLOR BEING THE OWNER OF A FLEET OF ICE CREAM VANS......

RECKONS HE OWES IT ALL TO ME.....

APPARENTLY I INSPIRED HIM WHEN WE WORKED TOGETHER AT EFFANDEE HOLDINGS, SOME YEARS BACK......

THAT'S NOT THE WAY I REMEMBER IT AT ALL..... IN FACT, I RECALL TRYING TO DISCOURAGE HIM WHEN HE TOLD ME OF HIS AMBITIONS...

I RECALL MY VERY WORDS... "DON'T GO INTO ICE CREAM" I SAID, "YOU'LL ONLY GET YOUR FINGERS BURNT...."

4.104

Bristow: Frank Dickens

THIS IS A GOOD ONE OF ME RELAXING IN THE SUN WITH A COOLING DRINK...

POSTBOY

LIKE IT...

HERE'S ONE OF JONES WATCHING THE GIRLS GO BY....

NICE ONE....

AND HERE'S ONE OF THE WHOLE GANG AFTER A HEAVY LUNCHTIME SESSION....

I DIDN'T REALISE YOU ALL WENT ON HOLIDAY TOGETHER...

HOLIDAY? WHO SAID ANYTHING ABOUT HOLIDAYS?

WE TOOK THESE IN THE OFFICE WHILE OUR BOSS WAS AWAY.......

4.25